SELF DISCOVERY JOURNAL

QUESTIONS TO FIND WHO YOU ARE IN 100 WRITING PROMPTS TO INCREASE SELF ESTEEM AND BOOST SELF IMPROVEMENT

BY MARY CASIE

TABLE OF
CONTENTS

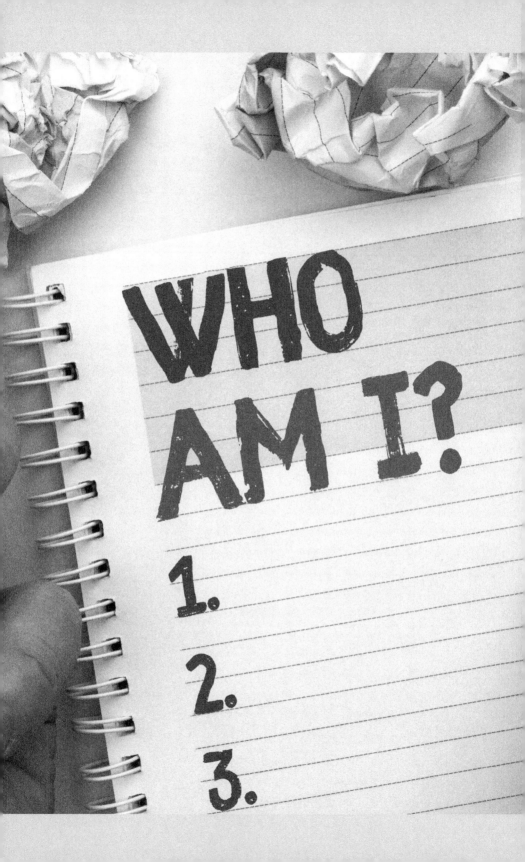

INTRODUCTION

A lot of people generally say that life is a long journey that every person needs to take. Whatever choices we make and whatever course we receive are, but a part of the appeal and mystery that our presence has. Self--discovery is an essential procedure that we must go through to understand the real function of his existence.

These might be challenging times. Looking into the inner being and finding the responses through reflection is the only method that one can get rid of such a problem. Most of the reasons why an individual is getting stuck in a particular location are when one failed to see it.

Although it holds that self-discovery may be a distinct process that each person might need to experience, what counts most is that in the end, we could not just discover who we are, however, the purpose of our existence and how we can make this existence a worthy testimony for others to be influenced by.

Therefore, numerous people have continuously found it efficient when they travel down memory lane and determine what they have done so far. They also found the most beautiful steps that they might require to deal with the next hurdle. Also, you will be able to find the experience you need to tread on by remembering and analyzing the things that have happened.

Most people can be lucky enough to have all the necessary information about how they have lived their lives. Some people may find this challenging, especially if they are among the people who have chosen to bury specific unwanted memories from their past.

Many people were able to make a self-discovery by linking the dots in their existence. One will never truly recognize the function of everything that has occurred unless he takes the time to stop in his tracks for a bit, recall, and see why those occasions came to pass and for what reasons they have to happen.

Most of us, often in the phase of experiencing getting confused, have no idea about how and why they came to such a point, and feel lost.These are the reasons why, sometimes, we don't know what to do and how we will react to it and move on.

Taking notes of things that we have experienced and would like to experience is the reason we motivate ourselves to do things. You will discover the answers you want to know or seek responses by writing it down in a journal. It will help you to discover yourself more and be mindful of yourself and your surroundings. Journaling towards Self-Discovery.

You might call your future dreams in your journal. They guide your choices and can help you to specify the kind of individual that you are and desire to end up being. There is no much better way to get to understand you than by getting to understand yourself than through your future dreams and aspirations.

I remember that when I was growing up, my diary was my best friend. It was the only place I could fully show myself in.

Do you really have a couple of people that you could talk to about your sensations? Do you feel risky discussing your real impressions? Do you discover it much more comfortable? You want to show your feelings and emotions to yourself?

You may want to discuss your feelings and emotions frankly and genuinely in your journal. This is especially the case for some of your uneasy feelings, something that every adolescent experiences from time to time. Remember, all of your emotions are all right for you because they are your sensations.

You might name your needs in your journal safely without another person criticizing it. We all have requirements, and many of them are unmet. So, don't put in the time to call your needs in your journal. Once you have requested them, you might attempt and bring about the ones that you believe that you require. Requirements aren't right or wrong. Needs are. The more you understand your criteria, the more you can understand them and tell others that you are dependent on them.

Journaling has many benefits... If you have a difficult time being sincere with your family and siblings about your feelings, it is time to start a journal. And keep in mind; you do not need to show your journal to anybody unless you genuinely wish to. Your journal is YOUR residential or commercial property.

If you keep your journal for about four weeks and refer back at the end of a month, the themes in self-discovery will become clear. A single day would remedy the exception of the other and make yourself to weigh all those various acts which are forgotten within no time at all needs to be included.

You are likewise not to think of any negative thing, let your mind think of just positive thoughts. In some cases, you may feel scared or sad; do not cast them away; however, instead, clinch on to them and look into the mirror and accept yourself the way you are.

Personal paper is the best way of self-discovery. You

can choose to keep a diary for just a week. You can put down quickly an overall series of work throughout that entire week. This will help you to examine themselves and be able to tell the state that they are in and make them think seriously about exactly what they are.

There were likely a few days when you didn't wish to write down your feelings or ideas, recall what was going on, were those days when you were stressed and harried, a situation in your life drew and was triggering a lot of stress and anxiety. Have you likewise seen other patterns forming that removed you from the stress factors in your life? That's what it's all about, being able to grow above the negative aspects of our lives.

You can utilize the typical books or get the not so costly notebooks from numerous shops. This will draw out the ideal look of the true you. Don't be scared of your thoughts, and if you wish to do this in a much easier method, you can consider sitting and taking a mirror in silence while closing your eyes and take note of your-self.

Think of how you look in the morning when you are dressing to fulfill the day—skim over your defects, your bulges, and saggy locations—now how would these look if you took an action class for a month.

Banish all unfavorable ideas, if you feel sad or afraid, embrace those sensations, open your eyes, and look into your mirror—"I enjoy you for who you are." When we can see ourselves and say those words and imply them, powerful sensations emerge.

Your journal can become your friend—we may lie to ourselves, play mind video games, but when you see your handwriting on the page and your real feelings popping out at you, your inner child protects and likes you unconditionally if you give yourself the approval to accept and hug the genuine you.

Utilizing a journal or blog site is an adventure inside yourself. You might believe blog site writing and journal writing are purely an egotistical move, yet this is a move inside yourself. A journal is not necessarily about writing that you took the pet for a walk today, however, what you believed during that time. Perhaps while at the supermarket, you saw an interaction between two people that made you show and pause. Believe in what you found out and why it is that you do particular things.

When journaling, it is best to choose a regular time, and this does not always indicate daily. Journal composing can be two or three times a week. You can blog in the early morning or night. It is best to stick with a relatively routine schedule so you can get into a pattern to composing and discussing at these times.

Are you sincere? If you are stressed about being honest about your ideas, make particular your journal is private. Hide your composed journal, and password safeguards an online journal.

CHAPTER 1

Benefits of Journaling

I believe that journaling can benefit everyone. The following are the benefits that you can potentially derive from journaling:

Benefits of Journaling

- Journaling helps you in self-discovery and to foster spiritual growth. You get to know more about yourself, who you are, and who you are not. Through journal prompts, you are invited to reflect on questions that you don't normally think of on a daily basis. You are also asked to trust your intuition and be open to allow for answers to arise. It's a holistic activity that engages all parts of you—the emotional, mental, your body wisdom, and the spiritual.

- Journaling is your invisible therapist, providing you with an opportunity to process your thoughts and feelings, thus reducing stress. It's how you can nurture your inner self and gives the suppressed part of yourself a chance to speak freely and safely. Detailing your thoughts and feelings with regards to a stressful event can be pretty much therapeutic. You are invited to release past hurts. Journaling brings about inner peace and harmony.

- Journaling helps you become a more effective communicator. By articulating your thoughts and emotions in writing, you gain the potential to become a better communicator in your relationships. You are no longer vague or play the avoidance card because you have not processed your inner world. Instead, words come more easily with balanced awareness. It potentially helps you to strengthen your relationships.

- Journaling helps you with greater confidence and boosts your self-esteem. With an increased understanding of yourself, you gain confidence. The exercise strengthens your core, providing balance to external influences.

- Journaling helps to clear up cluttered thinking. When you are too much in the head, you are unable to think clearly. Journaling offers you a way to get your thoughts out onto paper. As you review them on paper, you will find it a lot easier to come up with solutions.

- Journaling leads you to connect with your inner guidance. You will become much more aware of the beliefs and sabotage patterns that slows your progress, growth, and results. Through journaling your answers, you are asking your inner guidance on how you can make a shift.

- Journaling helps you with gratitude and positive thinking. You can use journaling as a way to help you focus on areas of life that you'd like to place attention on. One example is to do gratitude journaling. With gratitude journaling, you are expressing thanks for the blessings that you experience in your life. It's uplifting for your soul!

- Journaling helps you create a vision of your ideal life and potentially connects you with purpose. Through journal prompts, you prioritize what is important to you. You create a vision based on core ideals that inspires you to take aligned actions.

- Journaling aids in mindfulness meditation. If you feel that you are having a hard time meditating on a cushion because your mind can't keep still, try journaling for a start. Journaling invites you to go into a quiet space and be present with your thoughts and emotions, as an observer. Mindfulness journaling ultimately helps you reduce anxiety and stress.

- Journaling helps to support your health and well--being. Journaling benefits have been scientifically proven. Research shows that journaling

    o Improves cognitive functioning.

    o Decreases the symptoms of arthritis, asthma, and other health conditions.

    o Boost immune cell activity.

    o Reduce viral load in AIDS patients.

    o Speed up healing after surgery.

It's amazing how a simple technique can bring about

huge payoffs. Here's a one-line description that sums up all of the above…"Journaling is a low or no-cost writing therapy tool that can help you transform your life in the mind, body, and spirit, and from the inside--out." Evelyn Lim

Journaling: The Way for Spiritual Transformation

Journaling has helped me overcome anxiety and depression. During the course of writing, I was able to access greater joy, fulfillment, and creativity. Writing reflectively becomes an engaging experience that brings me calm, and amazingly, opens up a myriad of spiritual adventures.

Just imagine being able to access the benefits for yourself too. If you have forgotten yourself or can't find your true self, journaling can lead you to answers.

My wish is to help you so that you can be on your way to gaining insights, accessing deeper truths, and connecting with purpose.

Journaling puts you on an epic path of self-discovery. You begin from where you are by starting with basic questions before diving in to find the parts of you that you had left behind, repressed, or abandoned. A journaling review helps you to break down—shedding layers that do not serve you in your life and that do not reflect who you really are. Yet, it also involves a tremendous act of building up—recognizing who you can be.

Through journaling, if you find yourself identifying something that you'd like to change about yourself or effective strategy to achieve those goals is as important as the goal itself, increasing the likelihood of successful completion. When you write down your goals on paper, there is a psychological impact. Your mind sees this as an important activity, thus freeing up more mental space for you to think about and work on.

Helps Improve Memory and Cognition

According to research, writing creates distinct spatial regions in a person's mind, differentiating between important and not-so-important information, and thus exerting more effort to retain important stuff.

Helps You See the Big Picture

Writing a journal regularly, helps you see life as a whole. It will help you understand where we stand in this vast cosmos of experience and how brief life is. It allows you to see things truly for what they are, and not polished, sugar-coated versions of reality

4. Dream One Size Bigger

Perhaps the best approach to develop a probability mindset is to prompt yourself to dream one size greater than you ordinarily do. Let's be honest: the vast majority dream excessively little. They don't think sufficiently large. Make your arrangements as incredible as you like, because a quarter-century from now, they will appear fair. Make your arrangements multiple times as extraordinary as you initially arranged, and twenty-five a long time from now, you will ask why you didn't make them multiple times as fantastic."

If you drive yourself to dream all the more expansively, to envision your association one size greater, to make your objectives, in any event, a stage past what makes you agreeable, you will be compelled to develop. And it will set up your faith to be more noteworthy potential outcomes.

5. Question the Status Quo

A great many people need their lives to continue improving, yet they esteem harmony and steadiness simultaneously. People regularly overlook that you can't improve and remain the equivalent. Development implies change. Change requires testing the status quo. If you need more prominent potential outcomes, you can't agree with what you have now.

At the point when you become a plausibility thinker, you will confront numerous people who will need you to surrender your fantasies and grasp the norm. Achievers deny acknowledging the norm.

As you investigate more noteworthy potential outcomes for yourself, your association, or your family and others challenge you for it breathe easy because of realizing that at present as you read this, other probability thinkers the nation over and around the globe are thinking about relieving malignancy, growing new vitality sources, nourishing hungry people, and improving personal satisfaction. They are shaking things up against the chances, and you should, as well.

6. Discover Inspiration From Great Achievers

You can get intimate with a lot about probability thinking by examining incredible achievers. I referenced George Lucas here. Maybe he doesn't engage you, or you don't care for the motion picture industry. Find a few achievers you appreciate and study them. Search for people with the frame of mind of

I realize plausibility thinking isn't in style with numerous people. So call it what you like: the will to succeed, faith in yourself, trust in your capacity, confidence. It's truly valid: people who accept they can't, don't. Be that as it may, if you trust you can, you can! That is the intensity of plausibility thinking.

Feasibility Thinking Increases Others' Possibilities

Huge thinkers who get things going likewise make potential outcomes for other people. That occurs, to some extent, because it's infectious. You can't resist the urge to turn out to be more satisfied and think greater when you're around probability thinkers.

Feasibility Thinking Allows You to Dream Big Dreams

Regardless of what you're calling, probability thinking can assist you with broadening your points of view and dream greater dreams. "Huge thinkers are masters in making positive, forward-looking, idealistic ideas in their minds and the minds of others." If you grasp probability thinking, your fantasies will go from molehill to mountain size, and because you have confidence in potential outcomes, you set yourself in place to accomplish them.

Feasibility Thinking Makes It Possible to Rise Above Average

During the 1970s, when oil costs experienced the rooftop, vehicle creators were requested to make their vehicles more eco-friendly. One producer asked a gathering of senior specialists to lessen the heaviness of autos they were structuring. They chipped away at the issue and scanned for arrangements; however, they at long last reasoned that creation lighter vehicles weren't possible, would be as well costly and would display such a large number of security concerns. They couldn't escape the groove of their normal thinking.

What was the automaker's answer? They gave the issue to a gathering of less-experienced architects. The new group discovered approaches to decrease the heaviness of the organization's vehicles by many pounds. Because they felt that tackling the issue was conceivable, it was. Each time you evacuate the name of outlandish from an errand, you raise your potential from normal to of the diagrams.

Unselfish Thinking Brings Personal Fulfillment

Not many things in life bring more noteworthy individual prizes than helping other people. "Getters by and large don't get happiness; providers get it." At the point when you go through your day unselfishly serving others, around evening time, you can set out your head without any second thoughts and rest sufficiently.

In Drawing out the Best in People, There is no more respectable occupation in the world than to help another person to assist somebody succeeds."

Regardless of whether you have gone through a lot of your time on earth seeking after a selfish increase, it's never as well late to have a difference in heart.

Being Sincere Increases the Quality of Life

The spirit of liberality made by unselfish thinking gives people gratefulness for life and an understanding of its higher qualities. Seeing those in need and providing for the address that issue places many things into a point of view. It expands the personal satisfaction of the supplier and the collector. That is the reason I accept that there is no life as vacant as the self-focused life.

There is no life as focused as the self-void life. If you need to improve your world, at that point, concentrate on making a difference in others.

CHAPTER 4

Who am I?

Have you watched 'Kung Fu Panda 3'? There is a particular scene in this movie that strung a chord with me. Towards the end of the movie, the protagonist, Po (yes, the panda), figures out who he is. He realizes that he plays different roles in his life, and he is an amalgamation of all those parts. This is just about the best definition of who you are that I can deliver on this book without seeming too pretentious.

So, "Who am I?"

You may be a parent, a friend, a spouse, an accountant, a doctor, a traveler, a patient, or anything else. The truth is, you are a parent because you have a child. You are a husband or a wife because you are married. You are a traveler because you are on a journey. So, we all have different roles and identities, don't we? The task is to find the common essence found in all of these roles and identities.

How to Find Our Essence Among the Roles We Play

There are six building blocks of self-knowledge, and these are Values, Interests, Temperament, Around-the--clock activities, Life, and Strengths. You can use the acronym VITALS for these. These VITALS make up what you've come to know subconsciously as your sense of identity. They literally make you, you. Considering your VITALS will make your answers to the upcoming 200 questions that much more profound. So, let's begin!

Values

What things in life do you value? Out of those which values do you give more priority to? Your values could be anything like helping others, creativity, financial stability, staying healthy, and so on. Now ask yourself, what do you value most? Answering these questions will provide you with an ampler understanding of yourself.

By becoming conscious of your values, you will understand why you take the actions you take, what core motivations drive you, and the pillars over which you will build your life. E.g., you could be an introvert, but if you value leaving your comfort zone over self-expression, you may find yourself attempting public speaking overexpressing yourself through writing. And that's completely fine.

Interests

Interests would include anything that can retain your attention over prolonged periods of time. Your interests can include all the things you are passionate about your hobbies, or anything else that you find interesting.

There are a couple of questions that you can ask yourself for deciding what your interests are. What are the things that you usually pay attention to? What ignites your curiosity? What are your concerns? Your life will become quite vivid when you can focus your mental energy on something that excites and interests you. Understanding your interests will provide you with clues about the things that you are genuinely passionate about. All the successful people have found their success by doing things that interest them. If you aren't interested in something, then it is highly unlikely that you will spend any time or energy working on it.

Temperament

Temperament refers to your natural preferences. Do you feel you are more of an introvert or an extrovert? Do you thrive in social situations, or does it just make you feel exhausted? Do you like planning for things, or do you wish to take things as they come your way? Are you concerned with the minor details, or do you like big ideas?

The answers to these questions will help you in realizing the situations that will help you prosper. It will also help you in understanding all those things that you should ignore. Some love to be spontaneous, and then there are those who love to plan and then act deliberately. For instance, in the present world, spontaneity seems to be more valuable than planning. However, you don't have to opt for one over the other just because of the opinions that others hold. It is okay to go against the societal norm if it means that you are doing something that goes well with your personality. It is okay to be a planner if that is what you are comfortable with. The key to understanding yourself is acceptance.

Around the Clock Activities

What activities have you surrounded your daily grind with? Any repeated action becomes a habit, which eventually becomes something you end up building an identity around. What activities compose your life?

Make sure that the activities you engage in daily are making out of you what you actually want to become.

Life Mission

What would you do for the rest of your life, even if you weren't paid a dime for it? What would you regrettable thing not have done if you were to die today?

Think of your past. Remember what you wished to accomplish as a child, for instance. By recollecting such fond memories, you can get an idea of what you'd like to devote your life to. Do something different; it is never too late as long as it means that you are doing something that you like. Take some time and give it a real thought. It will help you in understanding yourself in a better manner.

Strengths

What activity or thing do people ask you for help in?

What abilities do you deem you're good at? What would others say you're good at?

Your strengths include your abilities, skills, and talents, but aren't necessarily restricted to just that. For instance, your characteristic traits like loyalty, comprehension, inclination towards learning, your IQ and EQ are all examples of possible strengths. Learn and grow your strengths so that you strengthen your sense of indivi-duality.

CHAPTER 5

How to Write a Journal

It is simple to write, really, it is, but that does not automatically make it easy to fill up the journal with details. While putting in the details necessary for answering the questions, you may need to confront realities that you may be uncomfortable with admitting, even in a private place like, in your journal.

When this happens, you may be tempted to taint the reality that you are about to write down just so you don't feel so bad or so guilty about what you're admitting. Here's the very first advice when using this journal; don't write untruths in this journal.

It'll be tough, but you have to make sure that you are being completely honest about the details that you're putting down here. Remember, it's your companion for this self-discovery path that you're on, and you don't want to be giving it false information; it wouldn't serve you well to do that.

Here's a list of do's and don'ts that you'll need as you start writing.

Don't...

- **Embellish:** write the reality as close to the actual way it is as possible. It's "close to the actual way" because there may be some small taints here and there due to the flawed nature of your memory, but there won't be anything to worry about as long as you retain the essence of the reality you're depicting.

- **Procrastinate:** If you don't know this already, you probably aren't as ready as you think you are to get on this path. Once you start, it's a commitment, and if you miss a day, you miss the point. So, really think about it cos this relationship between you and your journal isn't something you decide to call quits on.

- **Read the Whole Journal Before you Start:** (lol) it is tempting, but you'll like the surprises that the flow of the questions has better when you actually let them surprise you. In this journal, you can look forward to opening up a new issue that you know nothing about and look forward to answering it to the best of your abilities. Believe it, that simple reality of not knowing what to expect will keep you on your toes.

- **Forget:** To carry out a task that any question demands. Your success with this journal depends on your ability to follow through with the question of the day and any other demands it might have of you as you start your day.

- **Be Shabby With Details:** So you woke up late and can't really answer the question for the day as well as you usually do. Don't try to write abridged versions at all; it could come back to bite you. Instead, record an audio file as you hurry out and make a mental note to transcribe it as soon as you get a chance.

Do...

- **Your Best:** That's all you have to do. As soon as you get started, you'll need all the mental staying power that you can find to get back to your journal every new day that comes. There's no harm in starting small and taking the questions lightly and answering them in that way; matter of fact, the intensity of the questions builds up over time, and so there's enough room for you to get your groove on. You'll get the hang of this "journaling" thing before you know it, and you'll be happy you started it.

In this self-discovery journal, you should be willing to go all-in with details so that you can reap the most benefits. When you're able to follow the do's and don'ts, you'll always be best placed to get the most information about yourself out of the simple process of answering questions.

It is structured into months, and every day within that month has a question attached to it. You'll find quotes at the beginning of every month that you can reflect on throughout the month and whose wisdom will be reflected at various points through the questions that you answer during the month.

You must have the willingness to follow through with the questions in this journal until the very last day of the year,no matter how tough it gets. You may make omissions, but you'll make those omissions to your own peril.

Add "Journal Time" to even the most hectic schedules, and you'll make fewer omissions. When you cannot put words down directly in your journal, always make audio files; you may not have time to write, but you can always find time to squeeze in some speech that you can record.

P. S. Transcribe that audio as soon as your hands are free; whatever you do, make sure your journal is up to date with the information that each day requires you to answer.

As you start on this self-discovery path, I wish you the best of luck!

CHAPTER 6

How to Use Self Discovery Journal

The most challenging part of journaling, whether you are just starting or you want to start again, is finding your own unique voice, which is your own distinct journaling style, and then integrating it into your everyday life. Some people write down a couple of their immediate thoughts early in the morning or just before they go to bed at night. Other people enjoy writing for an hour every week, while some like to write during their commute to and/or from work.

Every person has their own journaling style, and every one of them is the "right way" of journaling. You have to remember that there are no set rules when it comes to writing in a self-discovery journal; you do you. You do not even have to stick to just one style of journaling; you can add pictures and other stuff some days while sticking to lengthy paragraphs the next. You can even write a short story narrating your experiences in the third person.

It is actually important that you try as many techniques as you want until such time that you find a routine that is sustainable, and most importantly, enjoyable for you.

Here are a couple of tips on starting a journal just so you can hit the ground running:

1. Find the Right Time for Journaling

Timing is the most important thing in journal writing. For instance, if you are a morning person, then it is probably best if you start writing in your journal at the break of dawn while everyone else in the house is still asleep. This is much better than trying to write in your journal before bedtime when you cannot help yourself from nodding off in the middle of dinner. Try writing at different points of the day, see which times you are more alert and motivated to write, and then devote a good chunk of your day just for writing.

2. Find a Spot Where You Can Write Without Interruptions

You will find it hard to collect your thoughts if there are too many outside distractions that are vying for your attention. Find a secluded place in your house where you can be sure to have at least half an hour's worth of peace and quiet so you can write in your journal. You can also go to your local park and looking for a secluded bench.

On the other hand, if you cannot find peace and quiet, you just have to make it on your own. Sit behind your desk, ready your journal and your pen, and then put on a pair of noise-canceling earphones or earbuds and play your favorite tunes; other people prefer listening to white noise or some music, choose which ones help you the most.

3. Keep Things Simple

At any single time, there might be dozens, maybe even hundreds of thoughts that are racing through your mind. This makes it hard to focus on what you need to write down in your journal. If you let your thoughts go unchecked, it will cause you to run into problems like writer's block, which means you will be wasting what precious time you have allocated for journaling without accomplishing anything.

To prevent your thoughts from going rampant, you should stick to a single theme every day. For instance, since Mondays make everyone feel a bit blue, you can use this time to work on conflicts that have been bothering you lately. On Wednesday, since it is the week-day hump, write about a lighter topic to help you get through the day.

By concentrating on a specific theme or idea per journal entry, you will be able to coordinate your thoughts and somehow clear your mind so that your ideas will flow almost effortlessly from your mind into your journal.

4. Get the Help of Friends

Everything becomes easier to stick to when you have people who are with you for the ride just as with any other habits,You have to ask your friends or family to join you, or better yet, to keep your anonymity, join an online journaling community. These online groups are composed of like-minded people who provide each other with support and encouragement.

Sometimes, these online groups also provide each other with writing prompts in case some of the other members have trouble coming up with topics to write about.

5. Ask Your Journal A Lot of Questions

You need to treat your journal as if you are talking to a close confidant. You should ask thought-provoking questions, and then wait for the answers to come naturally.

Some of the questions that you can ask your journal include:

"What events this coming month am I most excited about?"

"What are the things that I like about my hometown?"

You can even ask, "How do I start writing in my journal?"

You can ask anything, just as long as they are open-ended questions that would really make you think hard about the answers. Now, do not stress about answering the questions "correctly," with these kinds of questions, there are no right or wrong answers, there is only "your answer."

6. Write at Least 3 to 4 Times Consecutively

If you are just starting on your journaling journey, it will be hard to force yourself to write every day for the rest of your life. That sort of target is not only overwhelming; it can also easily unmotivated you from continuing.

Instead of giving yourself an incredible goal, you should start by giving yourself small, bite-sized mini-goals to make the task much simpler, and also more rewarding because you will feel great once you achieve your target. For starters, just aim to write in your journal at least three times in a row. Once you achieve this feat, you can up the ante by requiring yourself to write every day for an entire week, and so on.

7. Give Yourself Some Time to Introspect After Writing

Right after you write your journal entry for the day, don't immediately close your journal and tuck it away; give yourself a couple of minutes to really process the things that you wrote down. Read through the entire entry at least once and think about the reasons why you wrote it. Sometimes you will find something surprising in the thing that you just wrote, something that you might have written semi-unconsciously.

Reading your newest journal entry and thinking about it real hard will help you understand yourself much better. You might even discover things that you did not know about yourself, or hidden insecurity that only someone from the outside looking in would discover.

8. Write Because You Want To

Journaling should not turn into an obligation because if it does, you will lose motivation later on. After all, it turns your journaling into a chore. Do not demand too much from yourself, and do not be too hard on yourself if you missed a day, or two, or three. Journaling is imperfect, and there are no set rules or a "right" way to do it. Just write in your journal whenever you have the chance.

9. Create a Positive Feedback Loop

As long as you continue writing in your journal, use it as an opportunity to learn more about yourself, you will find that doing so will produce more momentum for your journaling practice, making you want to write even more. Your natural curiosity will get the best of you; the more things you discover about yourself, thus setting up a self-sustaining positive feedback loop between your conscious and unconscious mind.

10. Concentrate More on the Process Rather Than the Product

The most important purpose for writing in a journal is to express and keep a record of your thoughts and feelings. You should put more emphasis on the writing process; focus more on creating a constant flow of words rather than worrying if what you are writing is grammatically correct or if it is interesting to read. Your journal is for your own personal use, but if you ever decide to let other people read your entries, then, by all means, proofread and edit your work if you want. Better yet, use your journal entries as a source of inspiration or actual material for your other writing projects.

Another set of guidelines that you can use to help you with your journaling comes from the official website of the Center for Journal Therapy, just remember the acronym WRITE.

W—What are the things you want to write about? Think about the things that went on in your life; what are your thoughts and what you are feeling, or what you are striving for right now. Give your thoughts a name and put it into writing.

R—Reflect on your thoughts. Before you start writing, take a couple of minutes to stay still, take a couple of deep breaths, and focus on your task. You can use mindfulness meditation with this step. Start your sentences with "I" statements, like "I want," "I think that," "I feel," and others. In addition, try to keep your statements rooted in the present by using present tenses.

I—Investigate your thoughts and feelings by writing. If you feel as if you are running out of things to write about or if your mind is starting to stray away, take a minute or two to refocus your mind, review what you have written so far, and continue writing.

T—Time yourself. If you are a beginner at journaling, your goal, at least for the moment, is to write continuously for five minutes. Set a timer to go off at exactly five minutes, and start writing, and do not stop until you hear the alarm off.

E—Exit with a bit of introspection. Review your work and take a minute or two to reflect on what you just wrote. Conclude your entry using one or two sentences, preferably starting with "After reading this, I find that...," "I am now aware of...," or simply "I feel..."

ppointment. As we become fruitful in riches, influence, and health, we have the ethical duty to share this accomplishment by serving others. As we are allowed control, we are to use that capacity to deliver generous impacts, spreading the cooperative attitude all through the Universal. Think philanthropy work, giving cash to causes, volunteering time to the older. At the point when this power is used selfishly or to hurt others in, at any rate, the Law of Attraction expresses that the evil thought sets into place a string of misfortune, as it were. A case of this is the point at which somebody tells a 'harmless exaggeration,' and this transforms into a progression of more deceives stay quiet about the first, and the impact snowballs until the blameworthy party is uncovered, by the Law of Nature.

Saddle the Energy of Atoms to the Mind

"Believing is the main action which the soul has, and thought is the main result of reasoning," states Haanel. Control your thoughts, and just spotlight on positive, helpful ideas. The best approach to control your thoughts is through extraordinary focus and total tender loving care. Every one of the activities practices fixation systems to manage which dreams can come into the Mind. At that point, by picking the thoughts that are in a joint effort with our definitive goals of achievement and concentrating on the results of these thoughts, we can control our predetermination.

Here, the MKS broadly expounds on the utilization of cause and impact to each human experience and how the purpose is consistently the consequence of thought. The MKS depicts cause and effects as each idea is a cause, and each condition is the impact. People have an "inside" and a "without," though the Mind works for the inside, and the without is outside impacts and condition—this implies to control what is happening in the "without," we should initially control what is occurring on the planet "inside." The MKS proceeds to clarify that the explanation individuals experience issues in life is because of the convergence of a wide range of thoughts that scramble around in our Mind lost and disorderly, and the "numbness of our genuine interests. The extraordinary assignment is to find the laws of nature to which we are to change ourselves." at the end of the day, we assume to find what is our actual purpose in life, and we are required to attempt to remain on the genuine way without straying for demeaned accomplishment from thought processes, for example, insatiability, jealousy, desire, or outrage.

Rather than considering how we are consistently going to get rich and whining because we never can manage the cost of anything, we ought to be valuable in our thought. We ought not to sit around griping because it is an exercise in futility and does nothing worth mentioning. Instead, we have to consider approaches to help other people. This is because the MKS instructs us that the best way to have control is to give control to get it back ten times. The MKS proceeds to talk about the importance of "I" in our Mind, and the impact we have when we state "I am going to..." and neglect to finish this. We ought to continually finish a venture or under-taking once we take it on, and we ought to never stop if avoidable because this demolishes our self-regard. At the point when we can proceed with things without falling flat, we will have learned self-control, and this is simply the world. This is the world that we have authority over and must use to pick up control.

The ability to prevail in our external, or everyday lives, depends exclusively on the accomplishment of our inward world, the world inside our mind. And when our inner world is ineffective, or despondent, this manifests in our ailments and maladies. The MKS portrays every single illness just like an immediate aftereffect of our thoughts, and that all sicknesses and diseases can along these lines be restored or turned around by the intensity of our Mind. As such, we can think about ourselves healthy. The individual must focus on being healthy, notwithstanding, as opposed to on being wiped out. This is an aftereffect of the Law of Attraction, which expresses that misfortune prompts more noteworthy misfortune, so that if somebody harps on the infection and loss of health and joy, the person in question will just experience the ill effects of more sickness and trouble. In any case, if the individual opposes every single negative thought about the condition and disregards it totally, the healthy ideas can reinvent the cells of the body and execute off the illness.

Some harmful projects hated by Haanel that are identified with Mind and thought are clairvoyance, trance-like influence, and searchers of wonders or paranormal action. Telepathy is seen as a negative mental expression that produces destructive thought impedance. Any individual who attempts to control someone else's thoughts loses authority over his mind control. Subliminal therapy can likewise be more hazardous than great because the operator just as the member is losing their mental capacity to the next individual. Marvels searchers, individuals searching for paranormal movement and the individuals who perform seances are for the most part searching for an inappropriate sort of intensity, as in dark enchantment, and this opens up the universe of contrary consideration that is past the information or need of a solitary individual and ought to be disregarded well.

CHAPTER 8

Questions on Health and Wealth

Physical Health

• **My Definition**

o What is my definition of healthy? What words, thoughts, and feelings have I associated with the word health?

• **Let's Talk 'Sickness'**

o What words, thoughts, and feelings have I associated with this word? Am I a sickly person? Why or why not?

• **Creating A Roadmap**

o Where am I in terms of physical health? Where do I want to be? What's my ideal body or phycal state like? Write away.

• **Roadblocks**

o What's stopping me from getting there?

- **Love What You Do**

o If I had to choose my favorite physical activity, it'd have to be... Because... (Please no eating, sleeping, etc... You get the point)

- **Physicality and I**

o Am I a physically active person? Why or why not? What're some physical activities that you hate?

- **Do More**

o How can I start doing more? There's something regarding your health you should be doing more of. Now's the time to identify what.

- **You Are What You Eat**

o Describe the top 5 foods that you eat most often. Next, rate each of the foods you've written about on a scale from 1 to 5, with 1 being very unhealthy and 5 being very healthy. How healthy are your eating habits?

- **Time for a Hate List**

o List down all the foods you hate to eat. Next, like before, rate each of them on a scale from 1 to 5, with 1 being unhealthy and 5 being healthy. Found any correlations?

- **The Ideal List**

o Make lists of all the foods you love and are also healthy. How can you get yourself to start eating more of these?

- **The Health Mastermind**

o Where can you find people that have the body and health you'd want to have? Describe how spending time with them would radically change your physical state. Next, go out and find them.

- **Activity Evaluation**

o Make lists of all the activities you engage in throughout the day. Which of these activities add to your health? Which of them take away from your health?

- **A Message to Yourself**

o Recall a time you've tried to improve your physical health and eventually talked yourself out of it. Do you have something to say to your past self?

- **A Writing Prompt**

o My body is...

- **Limited No More**

o Jot down limiting beliefs you may have about health and wellbeing (e.g. I'm overweight because that's just the way I am). Next, write an action you could take to prove these beliefs wrong.

Mental Health

- **The Pursuit Of Happiness**

o What is happiness for me? How about in my life? Is there any reason of stopping me from being happy right now? What is it? How can I make happiness as normal as breathing?

• Thought Evaluation

o What are the negative thoughts that keep recurring in my head? What triggers these thoughts? What are the positive thoughts that keep me happy? What triggers these thoughts?

• Making The Shift

o How can I try to keep out negative thoughts and keep my mind full of positive thoughts? Is meditation an option?

• My Friend Fear

o We're all running from something one way or another. What's one thing you could be afraid of and are running away from?

• Giver Of Meaning

o Describe things that have happened to you that left a negative mark on you. Is there a way you could see those things in a positive light? If the saying 'every cloud has a silver lining' were true, how could it apply to the negative things you've experienced?

• Worrisome Worries

o Do you often worry? Describe a time in the past where you worried yourself senseless for something you forgot about a few days after.

- **No One's Perfect**

o Recall a mistake you made that you still haven't forgiven yourself for. Write yourself an action plan for moving on.

- **Forgive Thyself**

o Make a letter from your future self to your present self-forgiving you for what you've done.

- **Forgiving Others**

o Write a letter to those who've wronged you. If forgiving them meant moving on, would you do it?

- **Inner Chatter**

o What thoughts keep me awake at night? List them down and label them as either positive or negative.

Wealth

- **Money, Money, Money...**

o Define wealth in your own words. According to you, is wealth, good or bad? Do you want it, or is it something that repels you?

- **Judging Wealth**

o Some wealthy peopleare good and donate millions of dollars to worthy causes and work towards the advancement of humanity. Likewise, some wealthy peopleare despicable and deserve little of what they have. If you were wealthy, which would you be? What would you do with your money?

o If you had all the time and money in the world...

What would you do?

• Wealth Is Good When In Good Hands

o Wealth can be good when it provides security, when it gives you and those around you freedom of time, and when it's used to provide jobs for others. Taking this into consideration, is generating wealth a priority in your life? Am I comfortable with this place of priority?

• How Much Do You Need?

o Have a serious look at your finances. How much money would you need to make per month to live comfortably, provide security for you and those around you, and have the freedom to do the things you've always wanted to do?

• Wealth Blocks

o What is stopping me from achieving my desired wealth? Is it a mindset? Lack of motivation? Not knowing where to start?

• The Wrong Way To Make Money

o Are my wealth-creating methods misaligned with my life mission? E.g., people who can't fathom a life without the piano but are stuck serving customers at a bank.

• On Mastery

o What skills help me earn my income? What other skills do I have that I can monetize?

• **Sharpen Your Blade**

o What skills do I need to learn to earn more money?

• **Monetizing Your Passion**

o It's not something limited to millennials with social media followings. You can do it too! Can I convert my passions into a wealth-creating profession? If it were possible, would it worth dedicating at least a few hours a day to this pursuit?

• **Looking For Yoda**

o How can you go about finding someone who has already generated wealth or has monetized their passion? How can you start learning from them?

• **On Investing**

o What are the available investment opportunities that will help me get returns and increase my wealth over time? What's stopping me from learning about these opportunities?

• **Bless What You Want**

o Does it affect me if my colleague or neighbor or someone else earns more money than I do? Do I befriend them, and endeavor to learn from them? Or do I look at them in envy and ridicule their success?

• **How Bad Do You Want It?**

o What amount of time do I spend on wealth creation each day? Is making money a large part of my around-the-clock activities? Remember, action expresses priority.

The Chicken orThe Egg?

o What should take priority, your passion, or the way you make money?

• A Money Affair

o What's your relationship with money? Are you spending it all as soon as it lands in your pocket? Or do you save most of it and live below your means?

• Money Memories

o Describe your parents' (or guardians') money habits. Had they always fought about money? Or was money something abundant during your childhood? How do you affect your view of money?

• Debt Conciliator

o We have to make money an important part of our lives if we want to have it in abundance. Make a list of all the people that owe you money and haven't paid you back and make a list of all the people you've borrowed money from but haven't paid back. Which are you more likely to do, borrow or lend? Do you think it's about time to conciliate these debts?

• Financial Goals

o Do I have my financial goals in place? What are your financial goals for this and the following five years?

• **The Richest Man In Babylon**

o The secret to wealth building? Save up 10 percent of everything that goes into your pockets for future investing. Write down a plan that will help you save a dime of every dollar you earn. If that's too much, then start with a nickel.

• **Financial Denial**

o Am I keeping my financial problems hidden from others who can help me? Am I in denial of my money problems?

• **Mind Over Money**

o It's important not to focus so much on wealth creation to the point that you disregard completely every other area of your life. Describe a life in which you're hustling and making money while winning in other areas of your life simultaneously. What needs to happen?

• **Tracking Money**

o For the next 7 days, jot down every penny you spend throughout the day. It will show you just how much of a spender you really are.

• **Money Wisdom**

o What's the worst financial advice you've heard? What's the best financial advice you've heard? Why?

CHAPTER 9

Questions on Emotions

1. How insatiable are you?

2. How are you distracted by new and exciting ideas and activities?

3. How do positive options and opportunities absorb your attention and energy?

4. Do you consider yourself a "renaissance man/woman"?

5. What skills have you been able to learn quickly? Would you have valued these skills more if you had struggled to acquire them?

6. When have you struggled with what to do to define your life path? Where are you on this journey now?

7. How have you used staying busy as a way to avoid the painful things in life?

8. Do you feel like you can find what you are looking for in life, or do you feel the need to try everything to make sure you know what is best?

9. Do you ever try to experience many things in life as a cover for the feeling of not really getting what you want out of life?

10. How can you connect more with your present moment? What would help ground you in the present?

11. Do others wish you were more serious? Do you have a balance between your optimism and your ability to take things seriously?

12. Did you feel disconnected from a nurturing figure in your childhood? How did this affect you?

13. Were you somehow cut off from maternal nurturance at a young age? Did another sibling or crisis in the family take away from you getting the nurturance you needed?

14. Did you decide at a young age that you had to take care of yourself? What impact has this had on you?

15. How do you occupy your mind with distractions? What would it look like to silence some of that inner noise?

16. Do you feel an inner conflict between wanting to move on to greener pastures and losing the connections around you?

17. What is your relationship like with drugs and alcohol? Is it healthy or unhealthy?

18. How have you used romantic relationships to provide excitement and newness to your life? Have you hurt others along the way?

19. Are you materialistic? What kind of things do you splurge on that others don't?

20. Do you have any workaholic tendencies? How have you tried to combat them?

21. Would others describe you as blunt? How has this gotten you into trouble?

22. Do you have too many projects on your plate right now? What would it look like to focus all of your energy on the most important one?

23. What responsibilities do you find most burdensome?

24. Do you ever feel bogged down by the slow pace of others? Would slowing down yourself benefit you in any way?

25. Do you ever feel caught between your commitments and your desire to do your own thing?

26. Do you ever feel like you are leaving a trail of loose ends around you? How could you tie some of those up?

27. When do you get caught up in fantasizing about the future?

28. Do you find yourself half, committing to things in case a better option comes up? Has this hurt anyone around you?

29. How does the old adage "the grass is always greener" resonate with you?

30. When do you most experience FOMO (fear of missing out)?

31. How do you handle your boredom? Is this healthy or unhealthy?

32. How have you sought out temporary relief from your anxiety? How did this work for you?

33. How do you act as an "energizer, catalyst, or spark plug" in social situations?

34. Has your desire to make others happy had any negative consequences on you and your own happiness?

35. Do you feel the pressure to entertain, dazzle, and charm those around you? Do you find it satisfying, or does it feel like you have to put on a show?

36. How have you tried to fill your inner emptiness with external gratifications?

37. How have you kept your mind full in order to avoid your anxieties? How do you feel when you sit with uncomfortable thoughts?

38. How can you pursue choices that will give you long--term gratification instead of instant gratification?

39. Are you open to the advice of others? Whose advice do you most value?

40. What is your relationship like with money? Do you ever feel that your pursuit of pleasure gets in your way of being financially wise?

41. What is one way that you could slow down today?

42. How many partially finished projects do you have going right now? Is there one that you could finish today?

43. Does your overbooked schedule ever get in the way of you actually enjoying the things you're committed to?

44. Do you ever feel deeply impatient or frustrated with yourself? What brings up these emotions for you?

45. Do you ever find yourself looking at tragedies in a positive light to escape the harder feelings you might experience?

46. Do you have underlying feelings of frustration about different areas in your life? Do others view this as self--centeredness?

47. How does staying in constant motion help you to suppress feelings such as guilt, heartbreak, and regret?

48. When have you been impulsive? How has this affected you or those around you?

49. What are you trying to escape from in life? How has this served you?

50. How does the phrase "enjoy now, pay later" resonate with you?

51. Do you need more and more of an experience for it to be as stimulating as the last time?

52. Make a list of projects you started and completed, and ones you started and abandoned. Do you see any similarities in these lists? What enables you to follow through on a project?

53. When stressed, do you feel like you are the only one who can get the job done?

54. When stressed do you feel the need to educate others? Does your passion for the topics you bring up ever turn to critique or debate?

55. What are you most afraid of in life? How do you cope with this fear?

56. How could you let yourself more fully process hard feelings you come across in life? What would this be like for you?

57. Do you have "instant expert" syndrome? How does this serve you?

58. Are you able to find joy in everyday things? How could you start doing this more?

59. Do you have a meditation practice? If not, how could you incorporate this into your routine?

60. How does your joyful spirit impact others? Do you feel the need for this joyfulness to be seen and appreciated by those around you?

61. Do you have a sense of abundance about your life and the opportunities around you? Do the people in your life share this same outlook?

62. How could you slow down?

63. How could you cultivate a quieter and more focused mind?

64. "Fulfillment is not the result of getting anything; it is the result of opening ourselves up to our present moment." How does this quote resonate with you?

65. Is it easier for you to stay in your present moment or get caught up planning what your future could be like?

66. How can you experience more joy in your life? How could you give more joy to others?

CHAPTER 10

Question on Spirituality

1. Describe a moment that you felt connected with something greater than yourself.

2. Are we born with a purpose? What's an experience that made you feel that people did or didn't?

3. Have you experienced a miracle or any sort of awakening? If so, how did you see the world differently afterwards?

4. Is there a difference between being religious and spiritual? What makes you feel that way?

5. Do you think reincarnation exists? What do you think you could have been in a past life, and why?

6. What role, if any, do spiritual beings have in our physical world? Why?

7. How do you perceive the concepts of fate and destiny in your life?

8. How does fate relate to a higher power? Which do you think would be greater, and why?

9. What do you think the universe has in store for you? For humanity? For itself?

10. What does the universe represent to you?

11. Has religion played a role in your life? What did it do for you, and what did you do for it?

12. How does your family influence your spirituality? Do they believe in anything different? Why?

13. What do you think might happen after we die, if anything?

14. What does death teach us about life? Why?

15. For me, what does it mean to you to be spiritual?

16. How are you spiritually?

17. Write down your understanding of the difference between religion and spirituality.

18. What are your thoughts on reincarnation?

19. What do you feel certain about but can't explain rationally?

20. What spiritual aspects do you not believe in, and what are your thoughts on that?

21. What could be a good spiritual practice for you?

22. Write down everything you relate to God.

CHAPTER 11
Questions on Family and Friends

1. Is there a person in your life that you admire? Who is it? What do you admire them for?

2. Who is someone today who makes you a better person? How do they encourage you?

3. Who is someone in your past that made you a better person? What did they do that made you feel or be better?

4. Describe something that happened to you that felt defined you. What does it really mean that you allowed it to define you? What changed in you as a result of the experience?

5. Think about somebody that you think is successful. Do you remember them for what happened to them, or what they did?

6. What is one way that you've made someone else's life better? Even with something as simple as a thank you or a hug?

7. Describe a time when somebody looked up to you. What did they want to learn from you?

8. Who is somebody you've seen doing things meaningful to themselves? What do you think their schedule is, and how do they make time for the things they like?

9. Who in your life makes you feel confident or sure about who you are? Reflect on the last thing you did with them that made you feel that way.

10. What support system do you have? Is there anything they did that made you feel better?

11. When is the last time you reached out to a friend ora family member and talked with them about how you're doing? How did they make you feel?

12. Do you feel comfortable reaching out to friends or family when you want help? What help would they provide, and what would you hope for out of the exchange?

13. Are there people in your life who negatively influence you? Does it really make sense to continue letting them play an active role in your life? Why or why not?

14. What's the best thing a good friend has said to you or about you?

15. How have you brought value to your closest friend's life?

16. What is something that you can do to strengthen the positive relationships in your life? Are you able to

reach out to them more often, or express your appreciation for them?

17. What positive ways has the way you've grown up benefited you?

18. Who is an expert of champion in your field who you look up to? How well do you think they performed at the beginning of their journey?

19. In what ways do the people you look up to are self-reliant? What steps do you think it took for them to get there?

20. If you could change something about yourself, what would it be? What's the smallest step you could take to overcome it?

21. Describe a memory that you treasure. What made it so meaningful to you?

22. What role does giving play in the lives of people you would want to be? What do they do, and where do they draw the line when they stop?

23. What does a healthy version of you look like? What habits are the same, and what habits are different?

24. Who has forgiven you for a mistake that you've made in the past? What positive message about you, were they sending when they did that?

25. How do the people you look up to frame their problems? In what ways do they perceive the setbacks that make them more effective than they otherwise would be?

26. What are some of the things that make you beautiful?

27. What would someone who was attracted to you say that they liked it?

28. What compliments are the most meaningful to you? What situations were you in that inspired those compliments, and how do you put yourself in more of those?

29. How do the confident people in your life make others feel about themselves? What can you do to help others feel the same way?

30. What do you wish a best friend would tell you about you? What would it mean for them to say that to you?

31. If you made a friend going through similar problems as you, what advice would you give them to improve their situation? What worked for you, and what didn't?

32. Who are some people who you would like to reconnect with? What would you hope they would say?

33. Who is someone you'd like to send a thank-you note to? Write what the note would say below!

34. What's something somebody called you that felt really good? Why do you think it made you feel that way?

35. Who is the last person who made you laugh? What made the situation funny?

36. What's something you spent money on recently

that made you feel good? What's something you spent money on recently that didn't make you feel good? How did your expectations change the outcome?

37. What's something that you're looking forward to? What makes it ideal in your mind?

38. What's something that you would like to get better at doing? What would it feel like when you accomplish that?

39. What's an activity that you really enjoy doing in your free time? What makes it so enjoyable?

40. What time for yourself do you doduring the day or week to relax or decompress?

41. What does it mean to take care of yourself? How does it apply to your life?

42. List a few negative influences in your life that are keeping you from what you want. What could your life be without them? What could be your steps you may take now to mitigate their influence?

43. What are some things about you that you wouldn't want to change? What positive impact do you imagine those things would have in your future?

44. If you could spend one hour a day only doing one thing that you wanted to do, what would it be? What would you be able to accomplish if you spent several months doing it?

45. What role does learning play in your life right now,

and what could you do if you learned more about the things you cared about?

46. What's something that you can do that you can look back on in the future and be happy about?

47. If you were somebody that you loved, how would you treat yourself differently?

48. Who is somebody that you would like to meet? How do you think they'd be spending their time?

49. Describe a world that you would like to live in. What about your life that made you think about it that way?

CHAPTER 12

Questions on Relationships

If You Are Single and Looking For an Ideal Partner

- What specific attributes do I want my ideal life partner to possess?

- Am I expecting a Prince Charming to come to rescue me? Why or why not?

- What's the vision I have in terms of an ideal relationship?

If You Are Currently In A Marriage/Life Partnership/ Relationship That You Would Like To Work On

- Who am I? What am I like when I am with this person?

- If currently in a marriage /life partnership/relationship, am I happy? Why or why not?

- What is the biggest challenge I see in the relationship?

- Am I expecting my spouse to be the "provider" for the family? Is this expectation causing any issue?

- What is the one thing that I can do to bring the relationship to the next level immediately?

- What did I appreciate about this person when I first met him/her?

- What do I appreciate about my partner now? Specify at least 3 qualities.

- What were the past relationships hurt that I hold on to? Is there a need to let go of? What is it?

- What is the single biggest belief change I could make that would improve my relationship?

- What's the vision that I hold for us in 10 years?

- How can I introduce more love into my relationship?

- In what ways can I show up as a great partner working together to weather any storm or challenges?

- Whenever I feel irritated by my spouse, I know that he or she is triggering something that I think and feel about myself. What is it?

- If there is a 14-day romantic getaway that we can go to, where would I like this place to be, and why?

- If I am writing a letter to express thanks to my partner, I would say...

- I ask forgiveness from my partner for...

- What would a great level-10 relationship look like?

In Your Relationships With Your Children

- What can I celebrate when I think about my relationship with my child or children?

- My love letter to one of my children reads like this...

- Here's what I feel like saying to my child as a form of advice...

- I am thankful to my children for...

- I ask for forgiveness from my children for...

- How I would like to improve my relationship with my children...

- When I think about my children, I feel...

- I would like to inspire my children to...

- The values that I would like my children to learn are...

- My motivational "don't give up" speech to my children is...

In Your Relationship With Parents

- How's my relationship with my parents like? On a scale of 1-10, how do I rate my relationship with them?

- When I think about my parents, I think and feel...

- My gratitude letter to my parents goes like this...

- I would like to ask forgiveness from them...

- My happiest memory when I was a child with them is...

- My happiest memory as an adult with them is...

- To heal my relationship with them, I intend to let go of...

- What are the things that I can do to show that I care about them this week?

- If I can tell my parent (whether mum or dad) what I truly think and feel, I would say...

- What I would like to celebrate about my dad is...

- What I would like to celebrate about my mum is...

- The best things that they have taught me are...

In Your Relationships With Friends

- What friends do I enjoy spending time with? What are their qualities like?

- My "thank you" letter to my close friend goes like this...

- What do my friends describe me? What do they value in me?

- In times of trouble, who can I count on and why?

- How can I channel more love into my friendships?

- Who can I forgive whom I feel has wronged me? Write a forgiveness letter to this person.

- What are my views about toxic relationships? Am I in any right now? If so, how can I move away from these relationships and invest in the more supportive ones?

- What are my thoughts on friendships? What are my thoughts on having male and female friends?

32. Would I want to invest in agriculture?

33. What skill can I teach in 10 minutes?

34. What skill did I learn last year?

35. Is there any item that I have made myself?

36. What trade would I love to learn?

37. What futuristic innovation do I currently have?

38. What business idea do I have?

39. Of what benefit is the business idea to society?

40. How can I monetize such a business idea?

41. What would I manufacture if I had the funding?

42. How did I start doing the things I love?

43. Have I ever taken a break from the things I love doing?

44. What are the top 10 businesses I admire the most?

45. What are the top 5 career paths that are fulfilling to me?

46. What have I done to earn money?

47. Do I have a job?

48. How much do I get paid per hour on the job?

49. Is my job fulfilling?

50. Should applicants be encouraged to use family connections to get jobs?

51. Can one be guaranteed a job after college?

52. Do I need a job to succeed in life?

53. Have I ever been fired from a job? When and why?

54. Should family connections be used to get a job?

55. Would I quit my job if it does not align with my core values?

56. What professional skill am I working on this year?

57. What is my best productivity trick?

58. Who has made me better in my approach to work?

59. What led me to this career?

60. What energizes me at work?

61. What drains me at work?

62. How can I rate my manager on a scale of 1-10?

63. What are the biggest misconceptions that people have about my work position?

64. What work position do I aspire to attain in the next 2 years?

65. What would I love to add to the office?

66. Do I love my work environment?

67. Is my work environment spacious enough?

68. How effective am I at delivering my duties?

69. If I could instantly become an expert at something, what would that be?

70. What energizes me outside work?

71. What stresses me outside work?

72. Which talent do I possess that the world is in danger of ignoring?

73. How often am I dissatisfied with my work?

74. How often am I dissatisfied with my career?

75. Do I have a harmonious relationship at work? Have I found someone that can be considered as a best friend at work?

76. How often do I hang out with my best friend at work?

77. What jobs are within my group of options?

78. What career paths do I want off my list?

79. How do I want to be remembered at my workplace?

80. What impact do I want to make on the world through my career?

81. What do I spend my time thinking about when I am at work?

82. Do I secretly wish I had never shown up at work anytime I am at my workplace?

83. What do I have to offer my company or business?

84. What naturally comes to me when working?

85. How do I like to spend my work recess?

86. What are the biggest lessons I have learnt so far from my career?

87. What business goals do I want to achieve this quarter?

88. What did I achieve in my career today?

89. What issues do I face the most pertaining to organization and time management?

90. Am I easy to correct at my workplace?

91. Do I look for an excuse not to work at any given time?

92. How best can I communicate with my clients?

93. What can I do today that will bring me closer to my career goals?

94. What about my profession makes me proud?

95. What are the top 5 things I love about my job?

96. What field do I need to specialize in for me to improve on the job?

97. What is the next step in my career?

98. Can I achieve the next phase of my career from my current position?

99. If I can't achieve that, what plans do I have?

100. What are my greatest strengths professionally? How do I put them into good use?

101. What are my biggest weaknesses? How can I turn them into strengths?

102. What mistake this I make today, which I have learnt from?

103. How do I spend my time on a daily basis?

104. Would I need to adjust anything in my career?

105. What do I want my career to look like six months from now?

106. What action steps am I taking to make that happen?

107. What do I want my career to look like in three years? Five years?

108. What action steps am I taking to accomplish that?

109. What is my ideal career routine? How do I make that a reality?

110. When do I feel is the right age to begin a career?

111. Where do I go to each day after the workday ends?

112. How consistent is my paycheck?

113. Am I okay with my current paycheck?

114. What are my business hopes for this year?

115. When was the last time I used the word "busy" about myself?

116. When was the last time I used the word "stressed" about myself?

117. In ways can I make things easier for myself?

118. Do I believe in work/life balance?

119. What does work/life balance mean to me?

120. How can I achieve a perfect work/life balance?

121. What are the five heart desires I have for my career?

122. When was the last time I read a book about my career?

123. What were the five things I learnt from it?

124. How will I apply them to my career?

125. How has my performance been, being my own boss?

126. Do I keep myself happy, fulfilled, and motivated at all times

127. How can I use technology to advance my career?

128. Is my business scalable based on technology?

129. Does the use of social media enhance my career? How?

130. Does my work support the use of technology?

131. Is it possible to accomplish my 3-year goal in six months?

132. How can I make that happen?

133. Who was the first person that informed me about my career or job?

134. Have I had similar conversations ever since?

135. At what point in my life can I change a short-term temporary gain for a long-term game-changer?

136. What is my fourth most unique ability?

137. What is the worst-case scenario I would encounter if I take certain risks in my career?

138. How can I limit the downside to that?

139. What would I do if I was given $2 million, but would still have to work 35 hours a week?

140. Last month, did I often lag behind on sleep due to work? How can I correct that?

141. Was my free time affected last month due to work?

142. Did my personal commitments suffer as a result of work?

143. If I were my manager, would I be satisfied with my level of performance at work these past six months?

144. If not, what steps can I take to address these issues?

145. Did I achieve the career goals I set for myself five years ago? If not, why?

146. Did I maintain a steady relationship with my colleagues this past year?

147. If my goal is to be promoted, what steps have I put in place to ensure that happens?

148. Am I on the career path that I'm destined to be?

149. If I am not on the right career path, what changes can I do to correct that?

CHAPTER 14

100 Days Journal to Self-discovery

Day 1 __/__/__

Who are you?

....
....
....
....
....
....
....
....
....
....

Day 2 __/__/__

What Are You Most Gratefulfor In Life?

....
....
....

....
....
....
....
....
....
....

Day 3__/__/__

What are your values?

....
....
....
....
....
....
....
....
....
....

Day 4 __/__/__

What are the 3 biggest things you've learned in life to date?

....
....
....
....
....
....

....
....
....
....

Day 5 __/__/__

What advice would you have given to yourself 3 years ago?

....
....
....
....
....
....
....
....
....
....

Day 6__/__/__

What do you fear? How can you overcome it?

....
....
....
....
....
....
....
....
....

Day 7__/__/__

What are you worried about? Will it matter 3 years from now?

....
....
....
....
....
....
....
....
....

Day 8 __/__/__

What are your biggest goals and dreams?

....
....
....
....
....
....
....
....
....

Day 9 __/__/__

If you could do something for free for the rest of your life, what would it be?

··

··

··

··

··

··

··

··

··

Day 10__/__/__

What would you do if you knew you could not fail & there were no limitations of resources (money, time …)?

··

··

··

··

··

··

··

··

··

Day 11 __/__/__

What's stopping you now & how can you overcome it?

....
....
....
....
....
....
....
....
....
....

Day 12 __/__/__

Are you putting any parts of your life on hold? (Honestly)

....
....
....
....
....
....
....
....
....
....

Day 13__/__/__

What words, thoughts, and feelings have I associated with this word? with what word Am I a sickly person? Why or why not?

....
....
....
....
....
....
....
....
....

Day 14 __/__/__

Am I a physically active person? Why or why not? What're some physical activities that you hate?

....
....
....
....
....
....
....
....
....

Day 15 __/__/__

What are the negative thoughts that keep recurring in my head? What triggers these thoughts? What are the positive thoughts that keep me happy? What triggers these thoughts?

....

....

....

....

....

....

....

....

....

Day 16__/__/__

Describe things that have happened to you that left a negative mark on you. Is there a way you could see those things in a positive light? If the saying 'every cloud has a silver lining' were true, how could it apply to the negative things you've experienced?

....

....

....

....

....

....

....

....

....

Day 17 __/__/__

Write a letter from your future yourself to your present yourself forgiving you for what you've done.

....

....

....

....

....

....

....

....

....

Day 18 __/__/__

Write a letter to those who've wronged you. If forgiving them meant moving on, would you do it?

....

....

....

....

....

....

....

....

....

Day 19__/__/__

How do positive options and opportunities absorb your attention and energy?

....
....
....
....
....
....
....
....
....
....

Day 20 __/__/__

How can you connect more with your present moment? What would help ground you in the present?

....
....
....
....
....
....
....
....
....
....

Day 21 __/__/__

How have you used staying busy as a way to avoid the painful things in life?

....
....
....
....
....
....
....
....
....
....

Day 22__/__/__

Do you ever try to experience many things in life as a cover for the feeling of not really getting what you want out of life?

....
....
....
....
....
....
....
....
....
....

Day 23 __/__/__

Who is that someone today that makes you a better person? How do they encourage you?

....
....
....
....
....
....
....
....
....
....

Day 24__/__/__

Describe something that happened to you that you felt defined you. What does it really mean that you allowed it to define you? What changed in you as a result of the experience?

....
....
....
....
....
....
....
....
....

Day 41__/__/__

What limiting beliefs are you holding on to?

....
....
....
....
....
....
....
....
....
....

Day 42 __/__/__

What empowering beliefs can you take on moving forward?

....
....
....
....
....
....
....
....
....
....

Day 43 __/__/__

What are some bad habits you want to replace?

....
....
....
....
....
....
....
....
....
....

Day 44__/__/__

Where are you living right now? Are you in the past, future or present?

....
....
....
....
....
....
....
....
....
....

Day 45 __/__/__

What is your life's purpose? What is your mission?

....
....
....
....
....
....
....
....
....
....

Day 46 __/__/__

What drives you? Why do you wake up every day?

....
....
....
....
....
....
....
....
....
....

Day 47__/__/__

How can you make your life more meaningful starting today?

....
....
....
....
....
....
....
....
....
....

Day 48 __/__/__

How can you change someone's life for better today?

....
....
....
....
....
....
....
....
....
....

Day 49__/__/__

Who are the 5 people you spend the most time with?

....

....

....

....

....

....

....

....

....

Day 50__/__/__

Are these people holding you back or pushing you forward?

....

....

....

....

....

....

....

....

....

Day 51 __/__/__

What is your ideal life partner like?

....
....
....
....
....
....
....
....
....
....

Day 52 __/__/__

Are you afraid of letting others get close to you? If so, then why?

....
....
....
....
....
....
....
....
....
....

Day 53__/__/__

Who is the most important person to you in the world?

....
....
....
....
....
....
....
....
....
....

Day 54 __/__/__

Did you let him/her know how much you value their contributions to your life?

....
....
....
....
....
....
....
....
....
....

Day 55 __/__/__

What is your ideal career?

....
....
....
....
....
....
....
....
....
....

Day 56__/__/__

How can you start creating your ideal career starting today?

....
....
....
....
....
....
....
....
....
....

Day 57__/__/__

What is your ideal physical look?

....
....
....
....
....
....
....
....
....
....

Day 58 __/__/__

What do you need to do to achieve your ideal physical look?

....
....
....
....
....
....
....
....
....
....

Day 59 __/__/__

What is your ideal life?

....
....
....
....
....
....
....
....
....
....

Day 60__/__/__

What can you do today to start living your ideal life?

....
....
....
....
....
....
....
....
....
....

Day 61 __/__/__

What would you want to say to yourself 3 years in the future?

....
....
....
....
....
....
....
....
....
....

Day 62 __/__/__

Is there anything you are running away from?

....
....
....
....
....
....
....
....
....
....

Day 63__/__/__

Are you settling for less than what you are worth? Why?

....

....

....

....

....

....

....

....

....

....

Day 64 __/__/__

If you only had 1 year to live, how would you spend it?

....

....

....

....

....

....

....

....

....

....

Day 73 __/__/__

What can you learn from your biggest mistake to date?

....
....
....
....
....
....
....
....
....
....

Day 74__/__/__

What's a topic you need to learn more about to help you live a more fulfilling life?

....
....
....
....
....
....
....
....
....
....

Day 75__/__/__

Write 10 things you like to say no to:

....

....

....

....

....

....

....

....

....

....

Day 76 __/__/__

Write 10 things you like to say yes to:

....

....

....

....

....

....

....

....

....

....

Day 85__/__/__

Has anything changed your outlook on life?

....
....
....
....
....
....
....
....
....
....

Day 86 __/__/__

What cause do you feel strongly about? How can you help?

....
....
....
....
....
....
....
....
....
....

Day 87 __/__/__

Are you kind to yourself?

....
....
....
....
....
....
....
....
....
....

Day 88__/__/__

Are you a patient person?

....
....
....
....
....
....
....
....
....
....

CONCLUSION

The objective of these questions is to cultivate self-discovery and mindfulness and motivate you to make a move for positive change. Self-request places you in the unlimited authority of your success and individual advancement. If rehearsed consistently, it will, in the long run, become a programmed reaction to challenges in your life and in getting ready for goals you need to accomplish.

Self-questioning likewise drives you to turn out to be increasingly contemplative and to perceive what you are feeling. Self-questioning just methods are focusing on yourself. You focus on...

- What you are thinking.

- What you are talking.

- How you are acting.

- How you are feeling.

- What you are eating.

- What you accept.

- How you are responding.

- What (and who) you are drawing in.

- How you decide.

- What you are stowing away.

- What designs you are finding in your life.

- How your body is reacting.

At the point when you focus and question yourself, you are deliberately tuning in.

You proactively see yourself from the situation of your higher self, your internal coach, and when your higher self-watches your contemplations, feelings, choices, and activities, you are compelled to find an answer, make a choice, or make a move.

As the questioner, you are constrained to perceive whether the appropriate response you concoct lines up with the individual you need to be. Does it line up with your honesty, your values, your motivation, your enthusiasm, your spirituality, with the center of what your identity is? Possibly you won't know what your identity is or who you wish to be because your asylum's at any point characterized the best form of yourself. You likely have an instinct about whether your decisions, beliefs, and activities are either positive or negative, life-confirming or life-annihilating, quiet, or fostering. Focusing is a source of inspiration, and following up on a call from your higher cognizance is simply the way mindfulness and a defining moment in your development. You see, where you are not completely yourself, and you choose to transform it.

So for what reason do you truly need to pose these ground-breaking inquiries? From my easygoing perception of people, it shows up the vast majority of us long for self-mindfulness; however, relatively few can identify the aching, and questioning makes greater clearness and bearing. For those of us who effectively look for self-mindfulness, focusing, and being the questioner is an immediate course to accomplishing what we need in life.

Focusing necessitates that we simplify our lives; evacuate interruptions; concentrate on the present minute; train our "monkey minds" to watch as opposed to race; relinquish our "conscience self," recognize how we have strayed from who we need to be.

These things can be hard to do because we don't live in the general public and culture that supports focus. Everything around us attempts to pull us away from focusing on our actual selves. Be that as it may, we must be solid. We need to retrain ourselves and stay focused on the hunt.

What is the compensation of being restrained, getting familiar with ourselves, and staying mindful of our considerations, feelings, activities, and decisions? For what reason do we truly need self-mindfulness? We wear 't. Glance around, and you'll see that most people are unconscious. The vast majority aren't focusing. A great many people are forever diverted by their general surroundings.

We can get by without self-mindfulness. We can be successful. We can even be happy in part. However, we can't be completely ourselves and completely alive. We can't experience the profundities of euphoria, close-ness, authenticity, association, harmony, and satisfac-tion without always looking for self-mindfulness.

When you practice self-questioning, you will never again be happy with living on the outside of life or living a falsehood. As you acquire an increasingly self-mind-fulness, your experience of life will expand and improve exponentially. You will feel increasingly focused, quiet, and satisfied.

I recommend you keep on asking yourself the inqui-ries in this routine and notice your responses to them and how your answers develop after some time. Keep composing your answers and the moves you make in a diary and make notes about how your life has impro-ved because of these questions. You may even keep an "activity schedule" where you record the specific moves you need to make every day because of what you are finding out about yourself.

Printed in Great Britain
by Amazon